Where are the babies?

Beverley Randell
Illustrated by Elizabeth Russell-Arnot

Here is Mother Mouse.

Where are her babies?

Here they are.

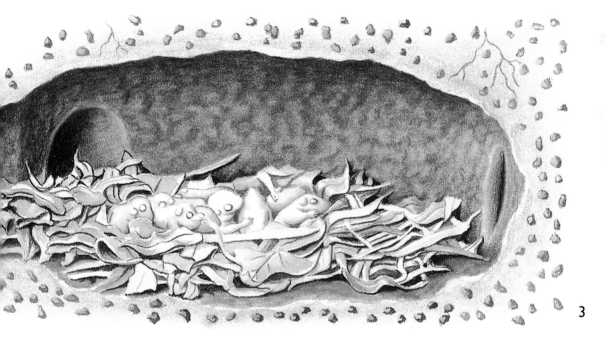

Here is Mother Hedgehog.

Where are her babies?

Here they are.

Here is Mother Rabbit.

Where are her babies?

Here they are.

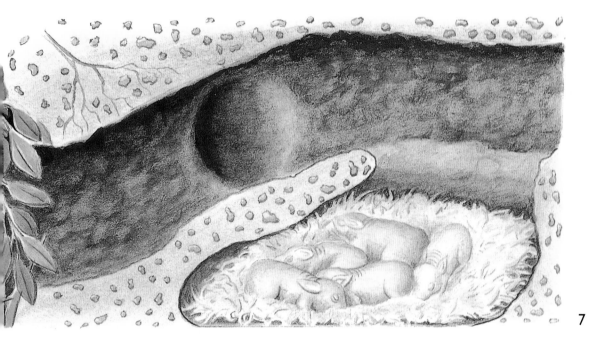

Here is Mother Fox.

Where are her babies?

Here they are.

Here is Mother Deer.

Where are her babies?

Here they are.

Here is Mother Frog.

Where are her babies?

Here they are.

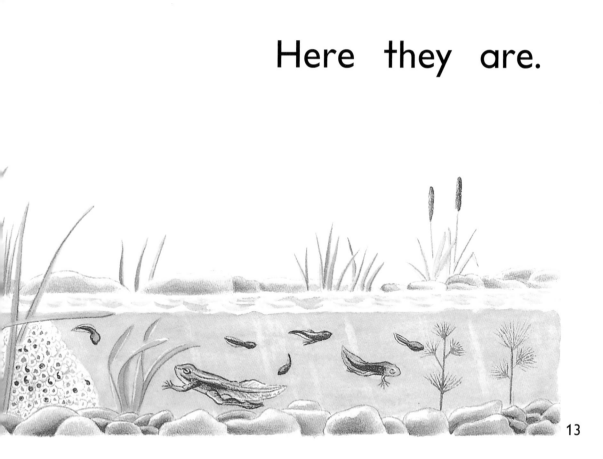

Here is Mother Kingfisher.

Where are her babies?

Where **are** her babies?

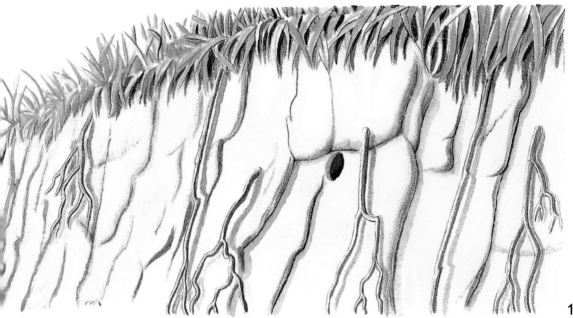

Here they are.

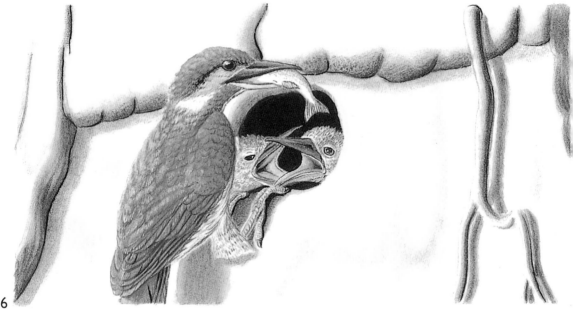